THE
SOUTH SUDAN
IS ON THE VERGE OF
FAILING

PROF MARTIN MARIAL TAKPINY

Africa
World Books
Pty Ltd

ISBN 978-0-6487937-7-9
© Martin Marial Takpinny, 2020

Published by Africa World Books Pty. Ltd.
(www.africaworldbooks.com)

Design and typesetting: Africa World Books

CHAPTER ONE

Pre-Independence Period

Juba conference in June 1947

A DECISION WAS MADE BY COLONIAL GOVERNMENTS IN KHARTOUM AND Uganda to carry out a survey among the tribes of Northern Uganda and Southern Sudan. It was by then a part of Anglo Egyptian Sudan, Sudan by then was a condominium that was being ruled by England and Egypt. The survey was to find out where the majority of the tribe along the boarder would be, the tribes were not to be divided between the two countries, the minority to be added to the majority in the other country.

The survey was to take place in 1939, fortunately or unfortunately the second world war broke out and it was given top priority by the governments of colonial power. The survey was shelfed, it did not stop from there, in Khartoum the constituent assembly made a ruling in 1945 that South Sudan should be united with Northern Sudan. A lawyer by profession, Mohumad Saleh Effendi. Shingeiti was told to go to Jubba to hold a conference to be attended by noblemen and chiefs of South Sudan. This conference came to be known as Juba Conference, where a decision was to be made. Mr Shingeiti told the noblemen and chiefs that the south has to be united to the north, the southern delegates did not like the idea, they simply said we can not unite at this time, we have to develop to be of the same level of the north and then we can think of unity. But Mr Shingeiti said we could not wait for such a time and at the same time the south could not be given a special status, we have to unite and the south to be treated as any part of The Sudan.

So, the conference had two opinions, one being championed by Mr Mohumad Saleh Eff. Shingeiti which was the unity and the southerner's opinion was not unite until the south was developed to the same level as the north and the conference ended there with the two ideas not coming together.

The Attendees of the Juba Conference were as follows:

J.W. Robertson, Esq., M.B.E.	Civil Secretary, Chairman
F.D. Kingdon Esq.	Governor Upper Nile
B.V. Marwood Rsq.	Governor Equatoria
G.H. Barter Esq.	Director of Establishment
M.F.A. Keen Esq.	Assistant Civil Secretary (Councils)
T.R.H. Owen Esq.	Deputy Governor Bahr El Ghazal

Mohd Saleh Eff. Shingeiti

Ibrahim Eff Badri

Kamyangi Ababa

Sgt. Major Philomon Majok

Clement Mboro

Hassan Fertak

James Tambura

Chief Cir Rehan

Chief Gir Kiro

Pastor Anderea Apaya

Chief Ukuma Bazin

Edward Adhok

Buth Diu

Chief Lolik Lado

Chief Lappanya

Father Guido Akou

Ciricio Iro

Chief Tete

Chief Luath Ajak

Hassan Eff. Ahmed Osman

Dr. Habib Abdalla

Sheikh Serur Mohd. Ramli

At that time The Sudan was preparing for independence and the Southerns were hopeful that if the independence came, they would get their share of representation in the government, their proportional share.

Independence came in 1956 and the south was not given to it what it was supposed to be given, the south was very unhappy and the north did not care the attitude of the south. Instead the north behaved as a conquering power, things did not go well and the south took to arms. In 1955 there was a mutiny in southern garrison of Torit and the mutiny spread to different parts of the south and that went on, lives were being lost, schools were being closed and there was some kind of war footing in the south

The north did not make good what they were saying, that there had to be unity. Instead very serious and bad incidents happened. There was a mass killing of innocent people in Wau, in juba and Malakal this was in 1964. The massacre in Wau was so bad it happened in a wedding party and almost all the officials who were in the party were killed by northern troops that were behaving like occupying soldiers. The few officials that remained during that massacre ran to the bush and the guerrilla movement started. The international friends of the south urged the Sudan government to make peace and there were negotiations going on in Addis Ababa, Ethiopia. In 1972 an agreement was reached that was known as the Addis Ababa accord.

It gave local autonomy to the South and the first Southerner to head this local autonomy was Mr Abel Alier Kuac, whom became the president of High Executive Council as it was called. But things were being controlled by Khartoum, who was to be appointed, who was to be dismissed, what is to be done in the south was being controlled by Khartoum.

All economic projects that were experimented and become successful earlier on were stopped, such as cement factory in Kapoeta, textile factory in Anzara in Yamboye, oil mill in Yoril, Sugar in Mangala, these were stopped and there was nothing going on in the south.

Mr Abel Alier Kuac was replaced by Mr Joseph Lago Younga, Khartoum was adopting this just simply to make sure that the South was controlled. It did not take long for Mr Joseph Lago Younga to be president of the High Executive Council, Khartoum removed him and another man was appointed Mr Abdula Rasas. A section of people would go to the president in Khartoum to tell him that their man has to be appointed as the president of the High Executive Council and he would except and tomorrow you would hear a different name.

After Mr Abdula Rasas, Mr Abel Alier Kuac was appointed a second time to be president of the High Executive Council. Things were not improving, there was discontent throughout, Mr Abel Alier Kuac was removed as president of the High Executive Council and Mr James Joseph Tambura who was appointed as president of the High Executive Council. He ruled for some time, when Khartoum came up with another approach to divide and rule, the South was divided into three regions and each region was further divided into states.

Mr James Joseph Tambura become the governor of Equatoria Region, Bahr El Ghazal region which was governed by Mr Lorance wol wol and upper Nile was ruled by Mr Daniel Kot Matthews and this was to divide and rule by central government in Khartoum. This situation continued for some time but senior officers from the south were very unhappy about the situation and they took to arms again. Mr Kerbino Kuanyin Bol Mutinied in Ayod in Jonglei state and moved to Bor and captured Bor. But the situation was quickly controlled by the central government and commander Kerbino Kuanyin Bol was chased away and ran into the bush.

Dr John Garnang de Mabior who was a Senior officer in the National Army in Khartoum was in the region of Jonglei at that time on leave and he was quickly recruited into the movement. Dr John Garnang de Mabior with two outstanding characteristics the ability to mobilize people and the ability to organise was then elected as a chairman and began to organise the movement. The movement was given the name Sudan People's Liberation Movement (SPLM) and formed an army to support its policies, the army was called Sudan People's Liberation Movement Army (SPLMA).

After this organisation of the movement Dr John Garnang de Mabior went around in Africa and abroad to explain the reasons for the movement.

As the central government was very active explaining to the world that the movement was just to disturb the government in Khartoum, that they had no good reasons for it and the central government was doing everything for the south. Dr John Garnang de Mabior put it upon himself that this propaganda could not be held by international bodies. He went on with the movement and was receiving help from friends and countries, Ethiopia gave the movement sanctuary. The movement was given facilities for a radio and the radio station was opened, it was called Sudan People's Liberation Movement radio or radio SPLM. This radio did a lot of work, it recruited people very quickly and SPLAM become a strong guerrilla army, which was very able to confront the Sudan Army.

SPLAM fought very vigorously and began to capture towns dispersing the national army when it moved from one town to another. As the movement become stronger international friends of the South convened a conference between the SPLM and the Sudan Government in Addis Ababa, unable to reach agreement this conference was moved several times until in Machakos Kenya a protocol was reached and signed. Becoming known as the Machakos Protocol, it was agreed that there had to be a plebiscite in the south. When Khartoum become aware of the terms it was very wild and the negotiator for Khartoum was blamed and almost put in prison, he fled the country to Europe.

Mean while the war was continuing in the south and the national army was staying only in big towns in the south, all the government officials moved to Khartoum with their families because the situation was very grave. Rural areas were controlled by the SPLA and the Government troops were staying in the towns and movement was done by the government army using convoys and in many cases these convoys were dispersed by the SPLM SPLA army. Later Dr John Garnang de Mabior made it known to Khartoum that there had to be negotiations while the fighting continued, as these two things had to go on simultaneously. An understanding between the Central Government and the movement could not be reached.

Other negotiations were going on by other movements that broke away from SPLM SPLA, especially the one led by Dr Reiak Machair, he negotiated in Frankfurt Germany and in Khartoum. But the main stream of the SPLM was the one really fighting. Other agreements were made and they were not executed. As time went on, the mediators between the SPLM and Khartoum Government pressed very hard on the two parties to come to an agreement as the war was becoming very expensive in terms of human lives. Admitting or rather a conference was called in Nibasha Kenya, where very serious discussions went on, the American government pressed very hard that an agreement must be reached and be signed, the government of president of George W Bush sent his envoy Cornel Paul to Nibasha to inform the conferees that they must reach an agreement otherwise an agreement which may not be to their liking would be forced on them.

Negotiations were very hard and difficult, at one point the chairman of Khartoum delegation just got up from the meeting and walked out and went straight to the airport to fly to Khartoum just to inform Khartoum that things were difficult, what could he do. Khartoum were aware of the consequences if there was no agreement reached, he was told to go back and to sign whatever he is given. He went back to Naibasha and a very important document was signed, which became know as comprehensive peace agreement, this comprehensive peace agreement was very detailed, but the important points were:

First there has to be an interim period of six years, after which a plebiscite has to be carried out among the southerns only and the southerns have to vote on two issues the first unity with the Sudan, the second separation from the Sudan, this were the main points to be carried out and the document was circulated to international bodies and circulated in the south and in the north.

And then arrangements were being made for a Plebiscite, this document was signed in January 2005. Khartoum was very unhappy and they wanted this agreement not to be implemented by all means. On the 30th June 2005 a helicopter crashed with Dr John Gurang and he was killed with all the people with him. It was a sad and dark day for the south. Things came to a standstill, the south was morning. On the contrary Khartoum and northern politicians were very happy they were almost dancing on the streets that Gurung is dead, they saw it as if that would be the end of everything, the end of the CPA which was to carry out the Plebiscite to let the south determine its own fate. It was not the case, as soon as the SPLM learned of the death late Gurung they went to the new site and they elected somebody to be the chairman of the movement and Salfa Kiir Mayardit was elected the chairman of the SPLM/SPLA.

The body of the Late Gurung was taken to Juba and was buried. President Youeri Kaquta Moseveni was a close friend of late Dr John Gurung Mabor, when he heard the news he drove from Kampala up to Juba to attend the burial. He was the only head of state that went there. After the burial he drove back to Uganda, he was a true friend of Dr John Gurung Mabor and a true friend of the south.

Things dragged on, first of all the plebiscite was conducted. Khartoum wanted to provoke the south to go to war again so that plebiscite could not be carried out. But President Salfa Kiir made the people not to fight and some of the officers were angry and wanted to fight, but he refused and said let's wait for the plebiscite, if we fight we will lose the plebiscite and the world and our international friends will not be happy with us. So, people listened to him and the plebiscite was conducted, both in the south and in Khartoum where the majority of Sothern's were and in the Diasspra all over the world. After counting the votes, before that there was an agreement between delegates from SPLM and delegates from Khartoum, the delegates from SPLM said that if the votes reach 50% + 1 that's enough for us to have our independence, delegates from Khartoum said it had to be 60% then you can have your independence. International mediators intervened, they say go for plebiscite what came out of it would be respected by both.

The south went for plebiscite 2010, when the results were counted and the percentage worked out the south and the world at large were surprised as they did not expect that the vote would go to that high percent. The result was 98.3% for separation of the south, it was a big surprise. Nothing was to be said again but the south has to go. After 64 years the south got what it wanted through plebiscite because this idea of separation was expressed by southern delegates in the Juba conference in 1947 so up to the time the South got independence in 2011.

Preparations were made to announce officially that the south has become an independent sovereign country called The Republic of South Sudan and the date was fixed to be the 9 July 2011. A compound was prepared and foreign dignitaries invited and people in the south moved to Juba to go and witness the important event that was to take place. On the morning of the 9th July 2011 people moved to the area where the celebration was to be held, foreign guests were seated and other important people. The population of Juba all went to that place and celebrations began. The flag of the Sudan was to be lowered while the flag of the republic of South Sudan was to be raised, one person was to do this but it so happened that two gentlemen were standing at the foot of the pole of the flag and both were trying to pull up the flag of the republic of South Sudan. These two Gentlemen were Vice President Dr Riak Machar and Secretary General of Sudan Liberation Movement Paganamu. They were struggling with the flag, Riak wanted to raise the flag Paganamu wanted to do so as well, this was the beginning of a dangerous struggle to come in the South, that led to a Civil War and the population was just looking at them. Eventually the flag reached its zenith and it was just playing with the breeze of juba, the old flag was folded and it was about to be taken to President Salva Kir but President Omar Bashir called for it and tried to take it but President Salva Kir grabbed it from him and he took it. Mean while a big boom 21 times was heard, this was a big gun saluting the new flag announcing the Southern Sudan to be an independent sovereign state, that was 21-gun salute to the flag.

After that another situation arose, marching music was played that was very popular to the population in the south, the music they would hear when a town was captured by SPLM SPLA. It was suspected that a unit of SPLA would come marching along the way track, but to the surprise of everybody it was not the soldiers marching the people marching were the amputees those that were lame some of their legs were cut off, no arm they were using crutches and then small boys of 11 years old dressed in Khaki were running along them or walking, it was an emotional seen. What was it for, it was to remind the audience that the republic of South Sudan was not given on a silver plate it was something fought for, a bitter war was fought and about 4 million people died to get this flag flying over Juba Town. It was quite emotional when these amputees came with these small boys, some people fainted some people wept openly. It was an emotional seen. Then the celebrations ended, Southern Sudan has become an independent country after 64 years.

During this time of war, the government in the south was managing its affairs, like making a budget from a sum allotted by the central government to meet the needs of the government in the south. There was no corruption and there was proper management of finance in the south, but a certain man posed as a contractor to construct a highway from northern Kenya to Juba Town and he said he was the Chairman of a company called "Tikma". He presented the whole cost of the construction of the highway and he demanded half of the total cost to start the work. He was given a huge sum of money and he went to Nairobi to start construction and that the project would last for about six months. It was hoped that such a situation would continue in a much better way as the south had become an independent sovereign country.

After one month there was no sign of that person, parliamentary investigation team was sent by the government to Nairobi to find the Chairman of Tikma. The investigation was given the name of Tikma Affair. The team found no trace of Tikma construction group. The report was presented to the regional assembly that there was no such construction company in Nairobi or any where in Kenya. That was the first and the last corruption experience in the Southern Sudan and the Tikma Affair was closed.

CHAPTER 2

Post independent period

Optimism

THE SOUTHERNS AND THEIR FRIENDS WERE VERY HAPPY AND VERY optimistic. The south felt that it would progress very vigorously with development of which it was deprived. It would start with development which was not done by Khartoum and was the source of their quarrel. South Sudan is a land full of natural resources just waiting to be developed for human use and this was the idea with the sourtherns, to start progressive development at all aspects of life, improve the roads make new roads build bridges, build schools, build hospitals, start agricultural projects, to produce materials for home consumption and export. This optimism was shared by some international friends and donors, donors made pledges and pledges of funds or materials for development. Some promised to build Hospitals which were badly needed, others were in for improvement and building of roads in the south especially the main roads such as Numaly Malakal road for instance. These were the projects, people sat down and prepared them but a situation developed the donors shied away from their pledges some were frustrated by some southern officials. They would come with a project and to start it, to be shown where to begin the work but some officials were asking for commission 10% or 25%. The donors were surprised, what for, why should they be given 10% this is a gift to Southern Sudan, they were frustrated and new things would not go well, so many of them went back to their countries and forgot what was supposed to be done in the South. So we the Southerner's had a hand in this situation where by many projects were stopped, pledgers were not forth coming and the south was unable to do anything without these foreign help. So, everything slowed down.

Out looking state, South Sudan was looking outside for something to continue with its progress, things became difficult. There was nothing being produced in South Sudan, everything was coming from outside, South Sudan became an outlooking State and unable to do anything for itself. No finance, no liquidity to carry out any projects. Loans and uncontrolled loans, some people decide to take loans very huge loans were given out, biggest loan given was $1.2 Billion and the least was $2 million. There were 46 people who took these big loans, there was no plan of getting the money back from them. For instance, there should have been a plan whereby the name needs to be recorded of the person taking the loan, his age to be recorded, the amount to be repaid per month and when the loan would end and of course this was not done. The loans were big such that if it was followed like that some loans would run for generations to be paid back, but this was not done. The money was taken and the treasury become empty. Some people that have little money instead of putting it in the banks in Juba they were invested in foreign banks in Nairobi and Kampala, no circulation of money in South Sudan which was a sad affair, money has to circulate inside. Many people were buying dollars in thousands and being hidden away. There was nothing left in the bank in terms of Southern Sudanese pounds or American dollars it all went, taken by Citizens it is a bad situation and a bad affair.

Students flock out also to Uganda and Kenya for their education, because no one was teaching them as teachers were not being paid, no money to pay them they have gone else where to find something to eat. Schools remain empty no staff, so students leave the country and Uganda and Kenya gave them help, they were allowed to go to schools to finish their educations. Some people started to move to Uganda and Kenya and live there, South Sudan was left and Juba Town become empty except foreigners because nothing to eat and life become very rough. Some people decided to rob people at night or even kill people to get what he has, that was the situation in Juba and other areas in South Sudan.

Corruption

Under these situations some people decided to take things of the government what ever little money was there it is taken and there is no accountability, so everyone was taking something here and there, it was difficult. Corruption become so bad, there was financial corruption and there was moral corruption. Financial corruption was taking the money where ever it is, moral corruption is writing the names of children and wives in the pay sheet so they could be given salaries. Women not working being paid, this is robbing the government. Another way of corruption was people being sent out for courses, given a lot of money to go for courses and, because some of them had no qualification, they could not do the courses. They came back as they went, knowing nothing. This is another form of corruption, money was given to that person and the person who made him to go gets part of the money, so there were so many forms of corruption going on. All the money being taken was from the Government Treasury while there is nothing going into the treasury, no revenue to the government. Even the Taxes were not being collected, taxes which are an important source of government revenue were not being collected from businessmen.

Grain Saga

The Grain Saga is a long-involved story of getting money from the government, so there were people transporting grain and their bills were containing millions of dollars or South Sudanese Pounds to be paid to them because they transported grain. You would see long cues at the ministry of finance people being paid of this money of which the grain has been transported to areas of hunger. This went on for some time with a lot of money paid out, in fact there was no grain so the name Grain Saga came up. The people doing this were known but no accountability, things were left like that and everything was chaotic.

Failed country

South Sudan is listed as a failed country, a failed country is a country with weak politics, weak economy and war this is exactly the situation such that Gross Domestic Production (GDP) is extremely low. Everything is chaotic, people are not being paid salary, people are hungry.

The Government is not asking when there is something wrong, instead there is a power struggle people are fighting. The situation between the two gentlemen when the flag was raised burst out in into an open war in 2016, there was serious fighting in Juba which spread out with many people killed. Weak politics, weak economy plus war made the country a failed country. The republic of South Sudan is a failed country, it meets these characteristics.

Failed Countries

Somalia	South Sudan
Syria	Iraq
Libia	Tunisia
Lebanon	Rwanda

The Republic of Southern Sudan was and is suffering from three problems. Ignorance, ignorance is a situation whereby officials do not know management of the governmental affairs. Two, corruption in its various forms as explained above. Three Tribalism some people would like to get their political objectives as a tribe instead of having a political party. The Southern Sudan has reached a stage of taking off, whereby people are to think of a party as a tribe. Any person has to get their political and social goals as a party member than a member of a certain tribe. The difficult situation of the southern government can be summarised as follows:

- Entrenched and rampant corruption
- Institutions of the government are severely undermined by mediocracy and the below average quality of education.
- Dismissal of Dr. Riak Machar from the post of Vice President that resulted to his rebellion

- The creation of the so called "Council of Jieng Elders ", which is seen by many as a body that works for the interest of Jieng at the expense of other communities
- Creation of central Uper Nile State to the exclusion of the Shulluk
- The murder of senior police officers in Yambio just before the independence
- Recruitment of "Mathiang Anyor"
- Indiscipline army and police force
- The problem of "unknown gunman", and the unwillingness of the government to punish murderers
- Domination of some government institutions by one ethnic groups
- Dura Saga

CHAPTER 3

Way Forward

THERE HAS TO BE CORRECTIVE MEASURES SO THAT SOUTH SUDAN DEVELOPS as expected. The corrective measures need a strong personality in the legislative, administrative and Judiciary. When these three pillars of government know what they are doing, things can be improved in a very short time. The corrective measures would be very meaningful if there is accountability and the right body to do that is the anti-corruption commission which did not work simply because the officials of anticorruption were being intimidated and they could not go on with their work. To improve its position it needs to be made a ministry of anticorruption and this needs to be headed by a very aggressive minister who needs to see that any person or any ministry or any commission not following the right way of governance concerning finance has to be presented to the Judiciary where proper investigation needs to be carried out and if found guilty to be punished accordingly. The President of the Republic of South Sudan has to supervise closely the ministry of anticorruption together with the Judiciary. This would be a very effective mechanism of making things go well, to see that proper management of financial affairs is carried out and the allotment of funds to projects is to be done according to financial regulations.

Another thing to be done is the ministry of agriculture to be impowered to make proper plans to let what is produced in Reng area for instance go to the world market, instead of storing the grain in the stores for years, a market has to be found so that when this grain is produced it has to go to the market to bring hard currency to the country. There has to be other product established by the ministry of agriculture for instance a pineapple plantation on a large scale in zandei area would be successful and productive project, with produce exported.

Experimental wheat crops to be experimented in Jonglei State and if successful produced commercially.

There needs to be a competition between ministries, especially the ministry of education, ministry of health and other service industries. A competition to give services to the people, any ministry that has succeeded in giving services out would be given a prize which needs to be worked out. So that the people in the ministry feel that their work has been appreciated. There should be many other measures to make sure that development is taking place. The old projects that were started, experimented and successfully completed, should be quickly implemented for instance Cement Factory in Kapoeta to produce cement. The south gets its cement from Uganda using a lot of hard currency, why not develop a cement factory in Kapoeta to produce a lot of cement which is needed in the country by both public and private sectors. This will bring money into the Government chest. People to be encouraged and given loans which are to be guided the amount to be given and the period when it should be repaid. And ask these people to come up with investments, another project that was experimented was kenaf jute in tonj which was successful and even the compound built and experimented but was stopped because of the war. This needs to be revived and continued with it. Another project was oil mill in Yoril, which produced oil. The people were encouraged to cultivate sim sim which they did to provide raw material. And get proper machinery, the machinery in Yoril was old type there should be a modern one now so as to produce oil and at the same time to produce soap. The oil which was produced at that time was distributed in the South and part of it was transported to the North, there were no such oil mills in the north or they were small. This project needs to be revived as the know how is there and won't take a lot of time. And people, rather than the Government should be thinking of digging Gold in Kapoeta and Yei areas. Foreign investors could be contracted to work with some South Sudanese to mine the Gold

There are a lot of these development projects that if people were to focus on them they would bring in revenue to both people and the government. The purpose of these projects is to create jobs for the citizens, the Southern Sudan has a large number of qualified citizens in the diaspora and there are no jobs in the country. South Sudan is a developing country therefore there is a continuous search for new jobs. The Government has to create jobs for its citizens. A lot of money is being spent on acquiring guns instead of generating developmental projects, any country that wants to help the republic of Southern Sudan should not give money but should come itself to design the project and employ southern Sudanese to develop it under their supervision. If money is given it would be taken by some officials and the project would die as so many projects have experienced in the past.

Important Dates

June 1947 - Juba Conference
3 March 1972 - Addis Ababa Accord
9 January 2005 - Comprehensive Peace Agreement
9 July 2011 – South Sudan gained independence

www.ingramcontent.com/pod-product-compliance
Lightning Source LLC
Chambersburg PA
CBHW032045040426
42334CB00039B/1285